THE TRIPLE GODDESS IN

OSCAR WILDE'S SALOME

MARIA L. ALONSO

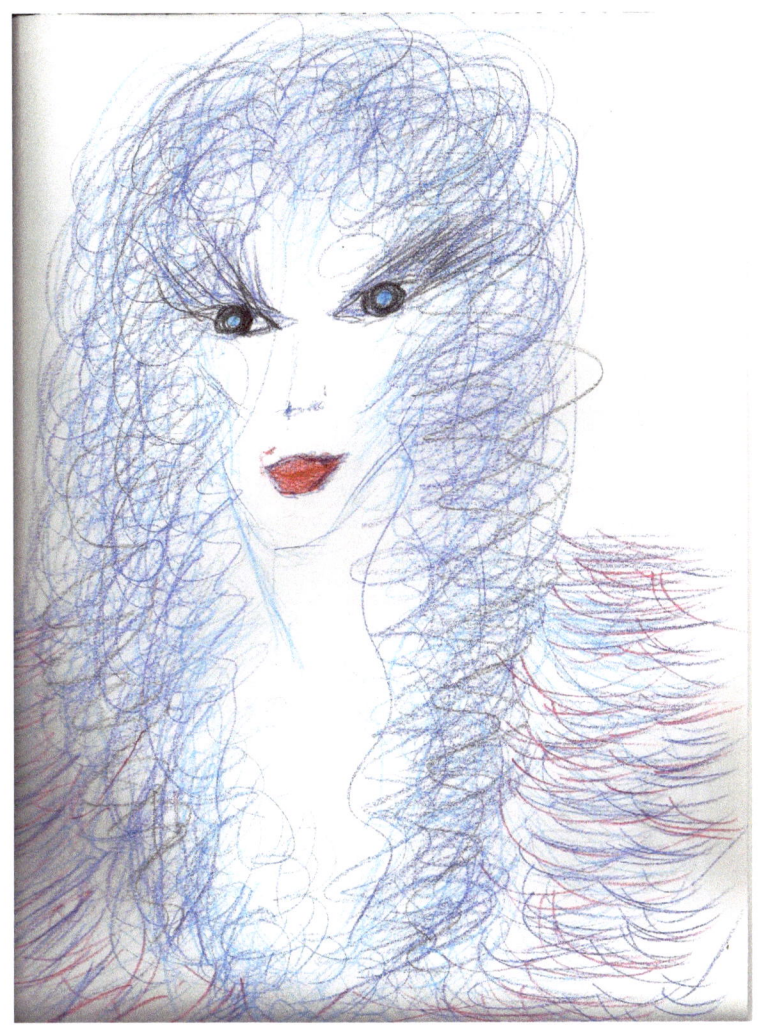

Salome – María L. Alonso

The influence of Lady' Wilde's studies on popular Irish literature is clearly seen in his son's writings where Celtic influence is present (1). His *Fairy Tales* show this with respect to the use of some "symbolic cromatism" centered on red, white and black.,

frequent in Celtic-origined poetry and connected to the image of a beloved person. Such as the example of Deirdre in The Death of Usnech's sons : thanks to the enlightening vision of a raven sucking blood within the snow, gets to know that her true lover will have raven-like hair, blood-like cheeks and snowy body (2), quite a similar image to that of Welsh Peredur's sweetheart:

> *"... her skin was whiter than the flower of the whiter crystal , while her hair*
> *and eyebrow were blacker than jet and in her cheeks were two little red spots*
> *redder than the reddest thing " (3)*

This imagery re-appears in stories like *The Nightingale and the Rose* . The protagonist, a young student who hopelessly searches for a red rose in order to conquer his beloved is described by the nightingale as dark-haired as the hyacynth, with red lips "like the rose of his desire" and pale-skinned like ivory.(5). Likewise, the only way of reaching his aim is by means of Death, through the nightingale's sacrifice : the bird will spill hos blood on a white rose at nicht whereas singing in the moonlight, stabbed by a rosethorn. We also find this symbolic meaning specially intensified throughout Salome.

Although Wilde chooses a subject whose cultural background is obviously different, the colours we have mentioned deeply evoke Celtic symbolism. We should also mention the omnipresent motif of the Moon , constantly associated to female characters and unmistakable allegory of purity, lust and death, which makes us immediately think of the representations of the Triple Goddess.

We must keep in mind that Celts used to establish a correspondence between the different aspects of Mother Goddess and the Moon's phases. The first one was the Maiden, symbol of purity and vital impulse, which was connected with the Crescent and whiteness.

Another aspect was that of the Mother or Mature Woman, fecundity, sexuality and plenitude, linked to the Full Moon and Red. And finally we have The Old Wisewoman,representative of Death, decadence and, nonetheless, wisdom and occult knowledge, related to blackness and the New Moon. In this play, the first aspect would correspond to princess Salome, the second, to her mother and the third , to Death itself, though this does not appear personified.

The moon of the Maiden Goddess, though may manifest herself full throughout the play, is individually evoked by Salome and her enamoured Syrian captain. Both refer to its linking to virginity and from that they both develop a series of metaphors which are unconsciously fused. Nevertheless, Herodias´slave´s point of view is drammatically opposed. He, in love with the Syrian, thinks that the Moon´s whiteness is a constant forethought of death.

That Red Moon perceived by Herod in one moment of the play is a crystal-clear image of his hedonist psychology and the sensuality simbolized by Mother Goddess – the Tetrarch sees the Moon as a drunken prostitute – and makes us think about Herodias' being constantly called a whore. Finally, the Old Hag or Death´s Goddess takes away the main characters of the play – Salome, Jokhanan and the Syrian captain . A short while before the tragic ending of the story the Moon grows darkened.

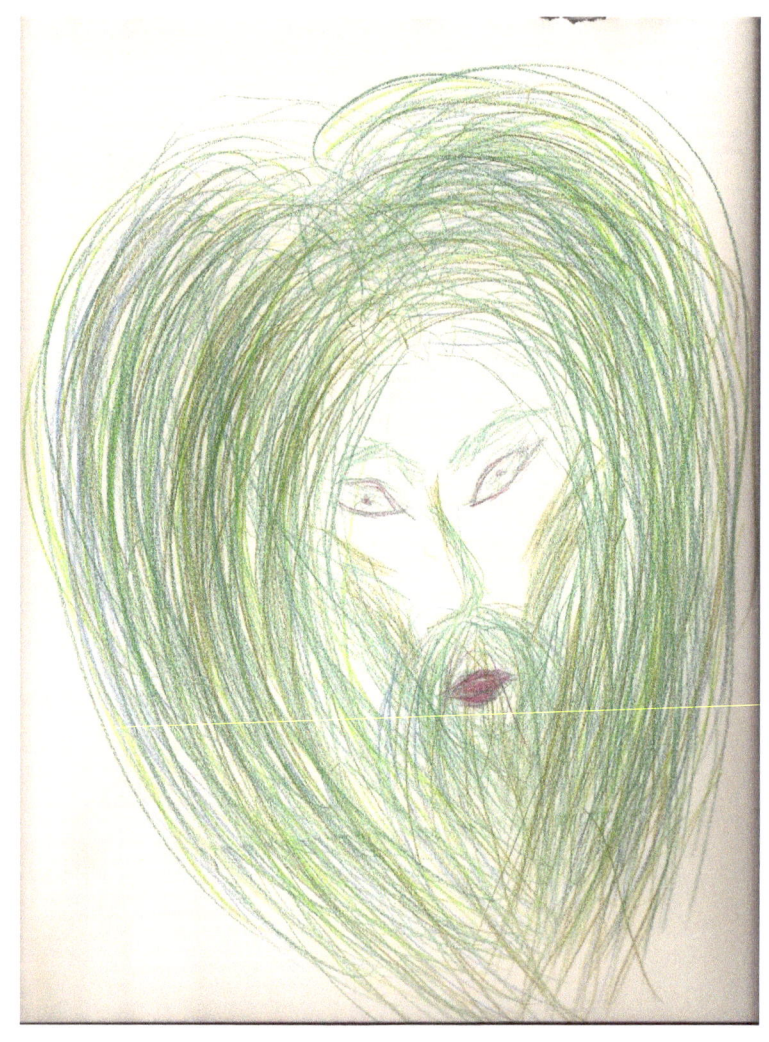

Jokhanaan- María L. Alonso

Manifestations of the maiden, the sensuous woman and the old death-bringer

The very first words of the play evoke Salome and the Moon – Death Goddess. They are introduced by Narraboth the Syrian:

"How beautiful is the princess Salome tonight!"

and Herodias' slave:

"Look at the moon! How strange the moon seems! She is like a woman rising from the tomb. She is like a dead woman. You would fancy she was looking for dead things!" (6)

Narraboth is aware of the prophetic value bestowed upon the Moon, but inversely, comparing it to Salome – therefore, to a maiden – and, unconsciously, anticipating the fateful veil dance. This contrast is depthened by the same syntactic structures his listener is using :

"She has a strange look. She is like a little princess who wears a yellow veil and whose feet are of silver. She is like a princess who has little doves for feet. You would fancy she was dancing,"

The page still insists on evoking the Moon as Death Goddess.

"She is like a woman who is dead"

Later on, Herod is also aware of the strange look of the Moon:

"The moon has a strange look tonight. Has she not a strange look?" (7)

Its influence is evident all through the play, so that it may be considered almost an outstanding character within the work.

The imagery linked to Salome by the young Syrian, always evoking purity – that is, the Maiden – remains all along the play like some sort of leit-motif, as it appears in the page´s omen-like words:

" How beautiful is the princess Salome tonight!"

"You are always looking at her, you look at her too much. It is dangerous to look at people in such fashion . Something terrible may happen"

Both characters make up a duet absent from everyone that surrounds them. Their manner of speaking, full of forethoughts, evoke some kind of uncanny, almost magical atmosphere around them , amidst that matter-of-fact conversation among the soldiers about Herod and the party.

"FIRST SOLDIER – *He is looking at something.*

SECOND SOLDIER –*He is looking at someone.*

FIRST SOLDIER – *At whom he is looking?*

SECOND SOLDIER – *I cannot tell.*

THE YOUNG SYRIAN –*How pale the princess is! Never have I seen her so pale!. She is like the shadow of a white rose in a mirror of silver. "*

THE PAGE – *You must not look at her"*

Y, más tarde, entre la conversación del capadocio, el nubio y los soldados:

THE YOUNG SYRIAN –*The princesa has hidden her face behind her fan, Her white hands are fluttering like doves that fly to their dove-cots. They are like white butterflies. They are just like white butterflies.*

THE PAGE –*What is it to you?Why do you look at her? You must not look at her (....)something terrible may happen"(9)*

Their trance-like attitude in front of the Moon involves a sort of mesmerized behaviour, reflected on the constant repetition of metaphors and syntactic structures. This makes us understand the concept of "magical atmosphere" we referred to before. Narraboth evokes

Salome with images closely related to moonly colours, white and silvery, that Celtic symbology related to magic and foreseeing visions – just remember that druids used to wear white and white mistletoe was held as specially scared. Doves and white flowers return when Salome leaves the hall.

YOUNG SYRIAN- *She is like a dove that has strayed. .. she is like a narcissus trembling in the wind... She's like a silver flower. "(10)*

And Salome herself takes back the Syrian's view: the Moon is a virgin, a silver flower, which she regards as a reflection of her own innocence. Indeed, a paranormal, almost magical atmosphere pèrvading them, amidst that down-to earth conversation between Herod's soldiers and the party.

FIRST SOLDIER: *-She is looking at something.*

SECOND SOLDIER - *She is looking at someone.*

FIRST SOLDIER- *At whom is she looking?*

SECOND SOLDIER - *I cannot tell.*

THE YOUNG SYRIAN - *How pale the princess is! Never have I seen her so pale. She is like the shadow of a white rose in a mirror of silver.*

THE PAGE-*You must not look at her....(12)*

And also later, amidst the conversation among the Capadocian, the Nubian and the soldiers:

THE YOUNG SYRIAN - *The princess has hidden her face behind her fan. Her white hands are fluttering like doves that fly to their dove-cots. They are like butterflies. They are just like white butterflies.*

THE PAGE - *What is it to you? Why do you look at her?*

This sort of maidenly feeling on Salome`s part can be deduced from her relief when finding herself in the open air, fram from the Tetrarch 's lascivious look and her admiration for the Moonly Goddess - Roman Diana - who

" ..... has never defiled herself . She has never abandoned herself to men like other goddesses"

This brief claim . some sort of declaration of principles, is obviously foretelling us how deeply, later on, Jokannaaan will impress her. Like the moon, he is *"cold and chaste"*. Salome could have fallen in love with him because all of him is an image of manly purity, far from that kind of manhood represented by her vicious stepfather and this courtly atmosphere that smothers her:

".... Jews from Jerusalem who are tearing each other in pieces over their foolish ceremonies, and barbarians who drink and drink...and Romans, brutal and coarse, with their uncouth jargon (13)

Really meaningful, the fact that the double invocation at the beginning of the play -the Moon, an ominous foresight for the page but evoking Salome`s image in Narraboth's voice - reappears just before Jokannaan's first coming on stage, love-striking Salome, the outcome of which will be the Syrian`s eventual suicide.

THE PAGE OF HERODIADES- *How strange the moon looks! You would think it was the hand of a dead woman who is seeking herself with a shroud.*

THE YOUNG SYRIAN- *She has a strange look!She is like a little princess whose eyes are of amber. Through the clouds of muslin she is smiling like a little princess (14)*

Initially, there 's some kind of striking antithesis about Salome's attraction to Jokhanaan. At first, she feels deeply shocked by his ruthless accusations against Herodias and:

" ...... his eyes above all... they are black holes burnt by torches in a Tyrian tapestry."

Black is, therefore, the first colour she uses to weave this opposition between attraction and horror, linked to ominous imagery from Celtic magical symbology. Indirectly, Salome evokes the face of the Hag , Death-Bringer:

" ..... they are like black caverns where dragons dwell, they are like the black caverns of Egypt in which the dragons make their lairs. They are like black lakes troubled by fantastic moons... (15)"

 After referring to dragons and those places considered as fairy dwellings (caves and lakes), the mention of the Moon`s magical identity establishes the contrast. All of a sudden, before Salome's eyes,Jokhanaan becomes:

"...... chaste as the moon is . He is like a moonbeam."

An, almost in the same way as Narraboth has done regarding her, Salome unfolds a wide range of evocations whose common link are moonly colours.

" He is like a thin ivory statue. He is like a shaft of silver. His flesh must be cool like ivory"

Later on, with her beloved one's lifeless head in her hands, she will remember that all of him was

"a garden full of doves and of silver lilies (16)"

Before dying , Narraboth will call her "*dove of all doves* " (17) once again.

The Moon´s magical atmosphere which previously surrounded Narraboth and the page now focuses on Jokhanaan before Salome's love-drunken eyes -"*Thy voice is wine to me"* – She then falls into a trance-like rapture, aloof from anything around except the prophet in whom she invokes the Triple Moonly Goddess symbolized by her different shades:

1)White

"I am amorous of thy body.. there is nothing in the world so white as thy body. Let me touch thy body"

2)Black

"It is of thy hair that I am enamoured ... There is nothing in the world so black as thy hair. Let me touch thy hair."

3)Red

"There is nothing in the world as red as thy mouth. Let me kiss thy mouth."

No doubt , a real mesmerizing atmosphere rises up through this constant repetition of structures:*"There is nothing in the world... Let me touch...."*

Thus , before Salome's eyes, Jokhanaan's moonly paleness is as meaningful as the Princess' for Narraboth.

" SALOME - *Thy body is white like the lilies of the field* (according to Narraboth, she was *"like a silver flower").....* the roses in the garden of the Queen of Arabia are not so *white as thy body.(*Narraboth would say*:"...she is like the shadow of a white rose"* (20)

Jokhanaan's aggressive attitude in front of Salome's devotion drives her magnetised surrender otherwise. Her opponent's peerless whiteness turns into a chain of deathly symbols.

"JOKHANAAN-"*Back daughter of Babylon! By woman came evil into the world.Speak not to me. I will not listen to thee.*

SALOME- *Thy body is hideous. It is like the body of a leper. It is like a plastered wall where vipers have crawled, like a plastered wall where the scorpions have made their nests"* (21)

His hair also gets transformed. After's Jokhanaan's second refusal ("*Profane not the temple of God* "(21) , that"*cluster of black grapes*" turns into a "*crown of thorns*" and a "*knot of black serpents*". Furthermore, this reminds us of the image of blacktthorn as an evil symbol within Celtic culture..

We have already pointed out the linking between the Triple Goddess' symbols and Salome's fascinated rapture. Obvious, the identification between the Prophet`s hair and Dark Moon`s Goddess

11

"The long black nights when the moon hides her face when the stars are afraid , are not

so black, The silence that dwells in the forest is not so black" (24)

Red -present in Jokhanaan´s lips - was the symbol of the Mother Goddess and among the

Celts evoked courage, violence, heroic qualities:

"....The red blasts of trumpets that herald that approach of kings and make afraid

the enemy , are not so red...(Thy mouth) is redder than the feet of him who cometh from

a forest where he hath slain a lion "

And also sensuousness:

"I will kiss thy mouth, Jokhanaan"

The Red Moon has also evident sexual symbolism in Herod's voice:

"She is like a mad woman, a mad woman who is seeking everywhere for lovers. She

is naked too (....)The clouds are seeking to clothe her nakedness...she reels through the

clouds like a drunken woman... I am sure that she is looking for lovers ...(25)

It is also a deathly omen, just before Salome's dance and Jokhanaan´s execution:

"HEROD - Look at the moon !She has become red.She has become red as blood. Ah,

the prophet prophesied truly.He prophesied that the moon would become red as blood.

Did he not prophesy it?" (26)

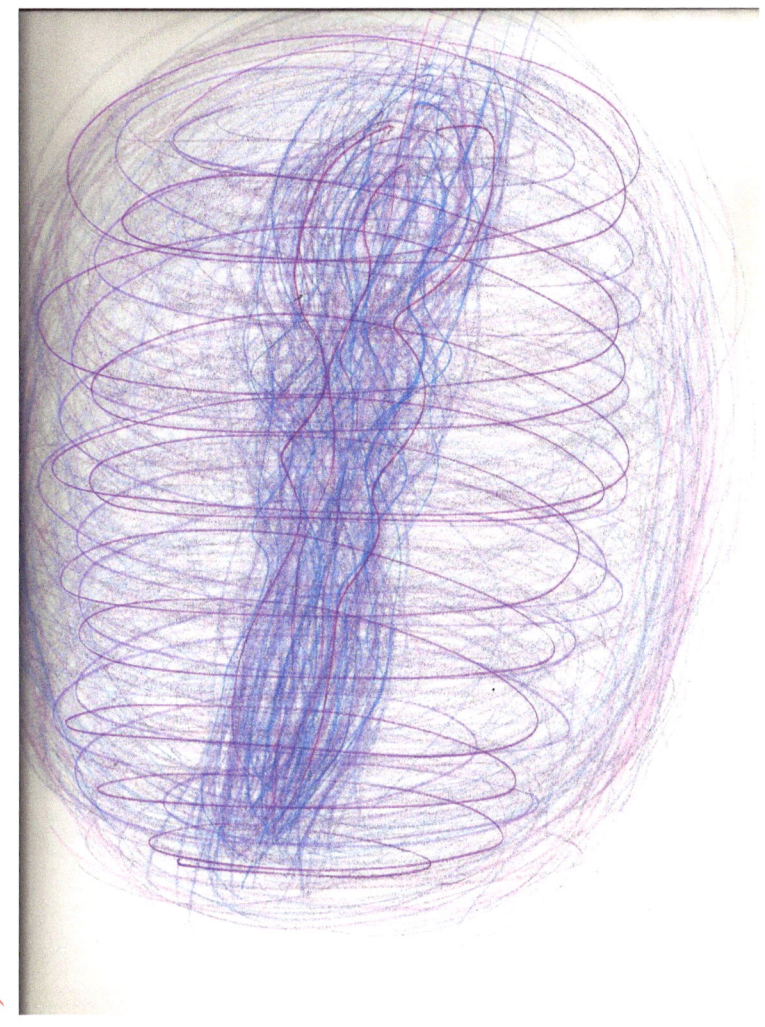

Dance of the Seven Veils —M.L. Alonso

Another persistent motif that heralds fatality is the "angel of death" perceived by Jokhanaan:

"JOKHANAAN- *In that day...... the moon shall become like blood... (27)* "

And also by Herod himself:

"HEROD- *I am sure I heard in the air a beating of wings, a beating of giant wings.....*"(28) .... " *There is an icy wind and I hear... wherefore do I hear in the air this beating of wings ?Ah one might fancy a bird, a huge black bird that hovers over the terrace* (¡¡¡The Great Raven, symbol of the Celtic Goddess of Death !!!)*Why can I not see it ,this bird?(29)*

Perhaps this coincidence might be symptomatic of some kind of synergetic connection between both characters that would somehow explain Herod's strong reluctance to fulfill Salome´s stubborn wish. He is willing to give her absolutely anything , no matter what - from jewels or priceless animals to part of his own kingdom or even the veil of Jerusalem's Temple - except Jokhanaan's life. That belevolence towards his prisoner is also manifested when he tries to excuse him before Herodias

"HERODIAS- *..... You allow him to revile your wife?*

HEROD - *He did not speak thy name.*

HERODIAS -*What does that matter?You know well it is I whom he seeks to revile.and I am your wife, am I not?*

HEROD-*Of a truth, dear and noble* Herodias, you are my wife and, before, that, you were the wife of my brother"(30)

When Salome finally gets her bloody prize, the concept of love as something magical and eerie, appears in Salome's voice. She sounds like meditating before her prey's lifeless face:

 "*Thy voice was a censer that scattered strange perfumes and when I looked on thee I heard a strange music...* "

But it is not that mesmerising sensation experienced before:

"*Thy voice is wine to me....the mystery of love is greater than the mystery of death....!"(31)*

The moon, once again, coordinates the development of the story. It is the divine Sorceress, the Messager of Death who manifests herself in the hidden Moon....

"*A great black cloud crosses the moon an conceals it completely*"

 .... which , for a second, shines back in triumph over Salome, just before she dies after quenching her desire.....

14

SALOME - *They say that love hath a bitter taste..but what of that? What of that? I have kissed thy mouth, Jokhanaan.*

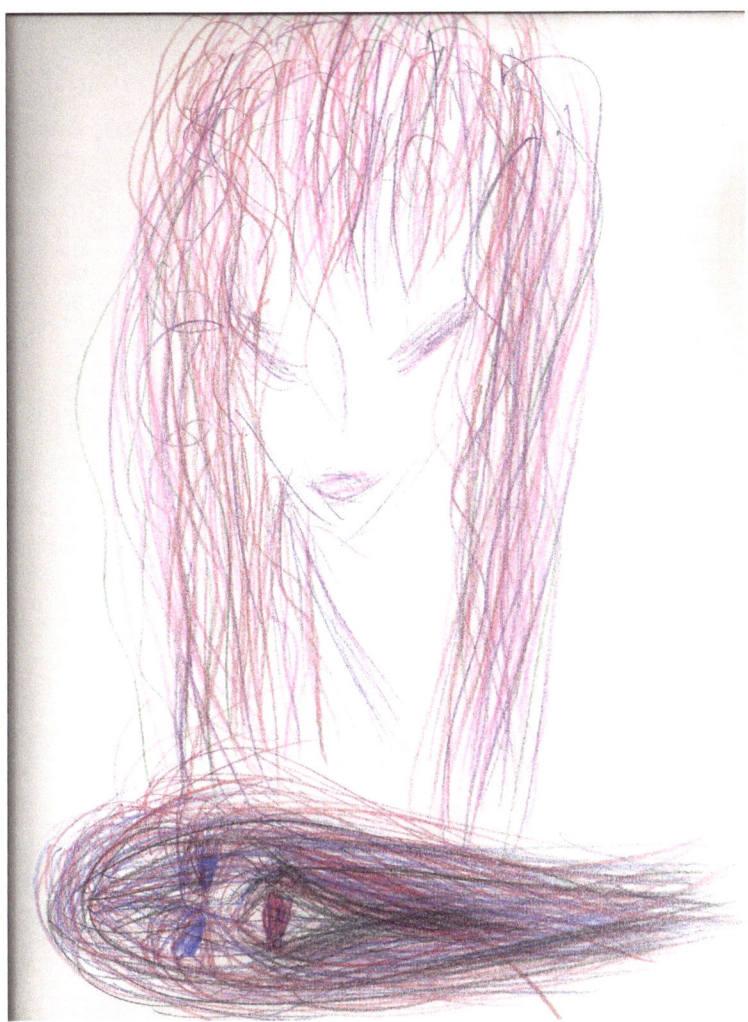

Salome & Jokhanaan — M. L. Alonso

15

BIBLIOGRAPHICAL NOTES

1)Oscar Wilde, *The Importance of Being Earnest and Other Plays.Penguin Books* (Harmmondsworth, 1972)

2) Lady Francesca Esperanza Wilde, *Ancient Legends of Ireland (*London, 1888)

3) JEAN MARKALE in *La Femme Celte (Payot: Paris 1972)p. 313.*

4) *Mabinogion,* trad. por JEFFREY GANTZ Penguin Books(Harmmondsworth. 1976) p.228.

5)*The Happy Prince and Other Stories.* Penguin Book*s (*Harmmondsworth 1994) 23-24.

6) See ROBERT GRAVES *La Diosa Blanca.* Farrar,Straus & Giroux *(*NYC:2007) y DJ.CONWAY *Celtic Magic,* Llewellyn Worldwide *(*1990)

7) O.WILDE *The Importance of Being Earnest and Other Plays ,* 319

8) M.ZIMMER , *The Mists of Avalon .* Penguin Books (Harmmondswoth, 1983)p.330

9) *O WILDE,* op,cit.. 320

10)*Ibidem,* 320.

11) " 322

12) " 320

13) " 322

14) " 325

15) " 326

16) " 346

17) " 328

18) " 327

19) " 328

20) " 327

21) " 327

22) " 327

23) " 328

24) " 328

25) " 330

26) " 340

27) · 336

28) " 338

29) " 339

30) " 336

31) " 347

"The Goddess Gallery" is a space where you can discover different shades and faces of female living force, with all its magical trascendence and archetypal force, that one which was once reflected in ancient sacred celebrations, those which were meant to enhance fertility .Such were Samhain (the beginning of the dark season) Jmbolc (the starting point of the bright days) Beltaine (the celebration of life, fire and sensuousness) and Lughnassad (the Thanksgiving rites for the reap of a lustful crop) J have alsop includes some other representative aspects of female divine archetype, those linked to the Virgin Mary and Jtalian *befana.*

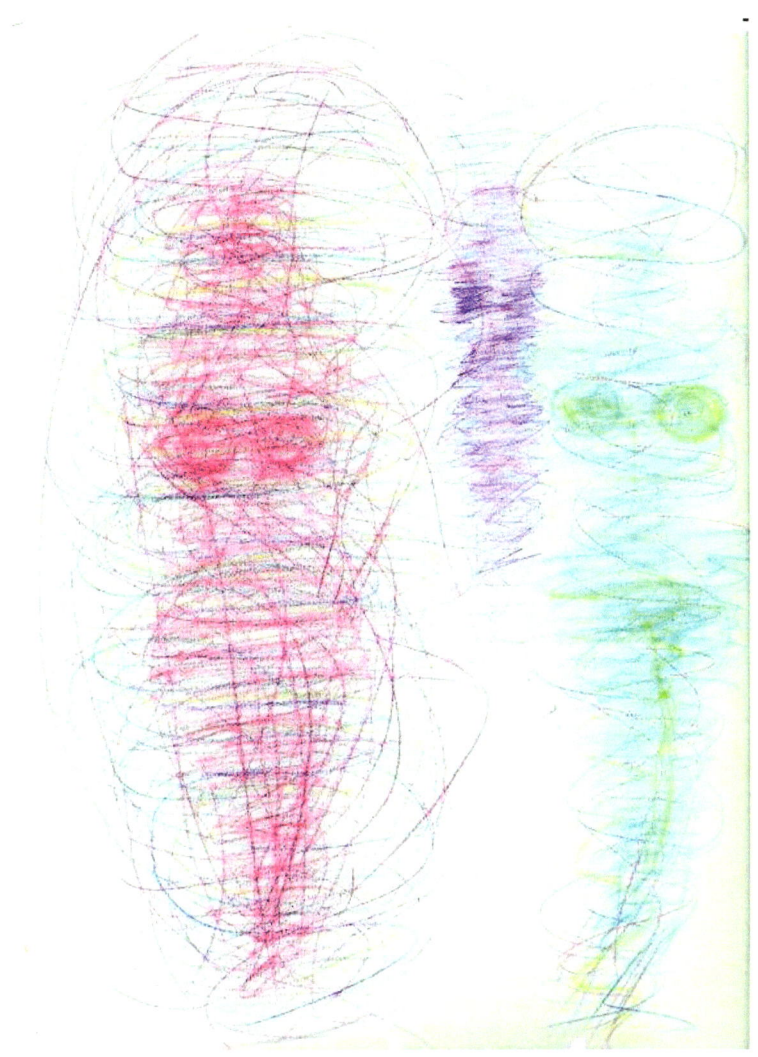

The Triple Goddess (M.L. Alonso)

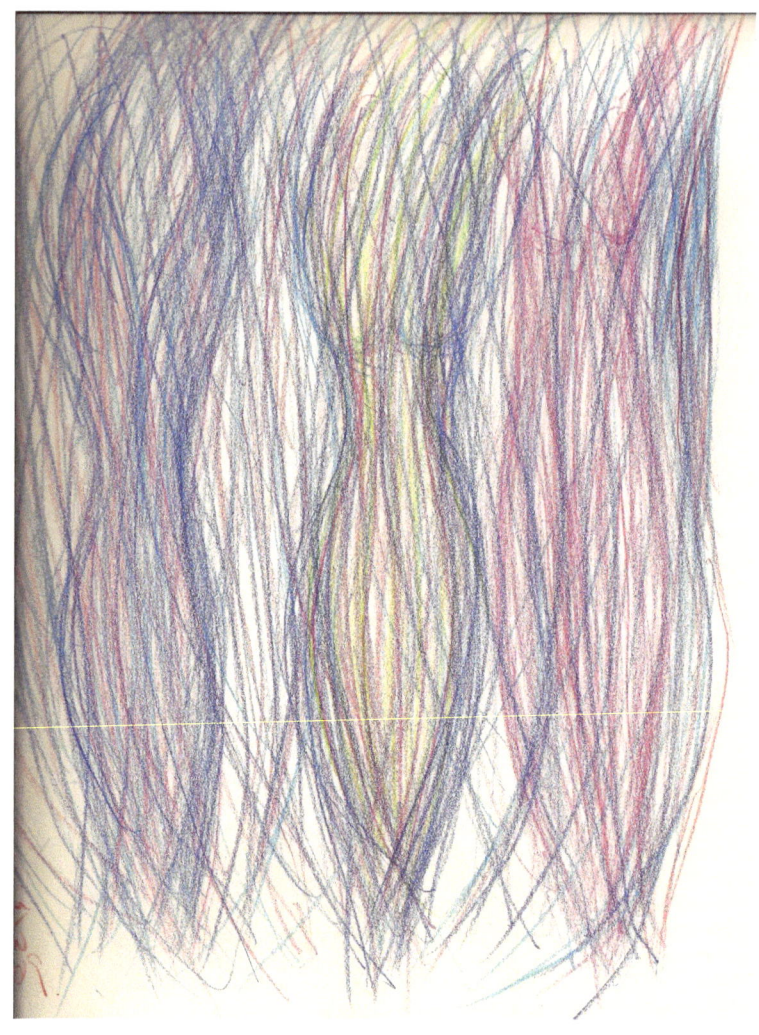

The Triple Goddess in Florence (M. L. Alonso)

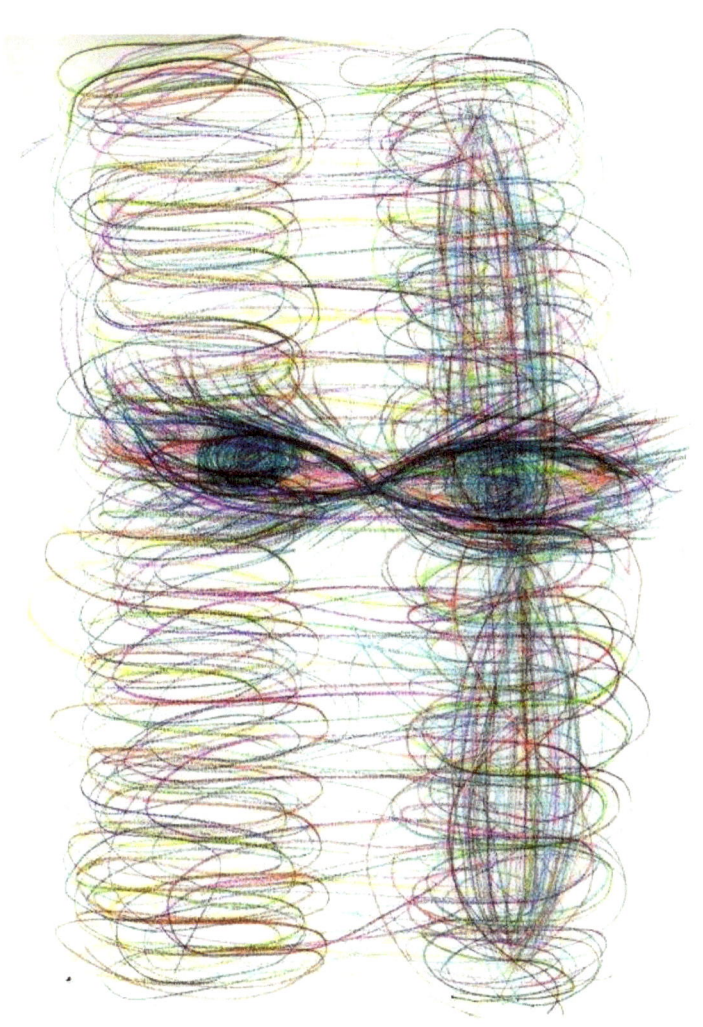

The Weaving Goddess (M. L. Alonso)

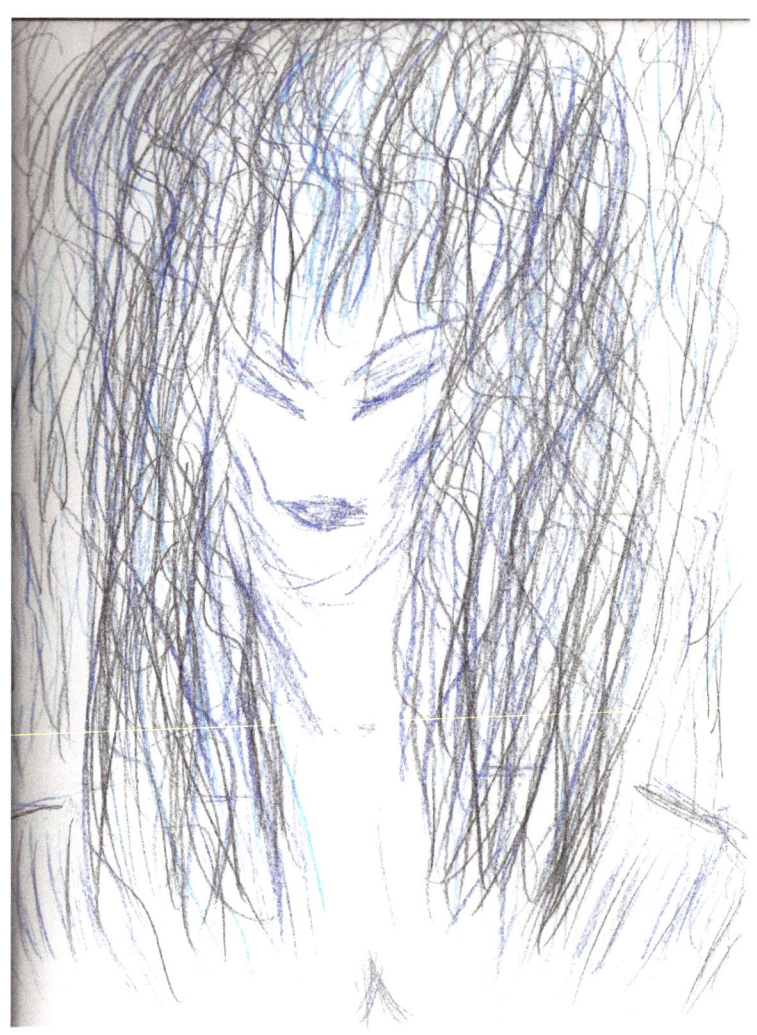

Samhain (M.L. Alonso)

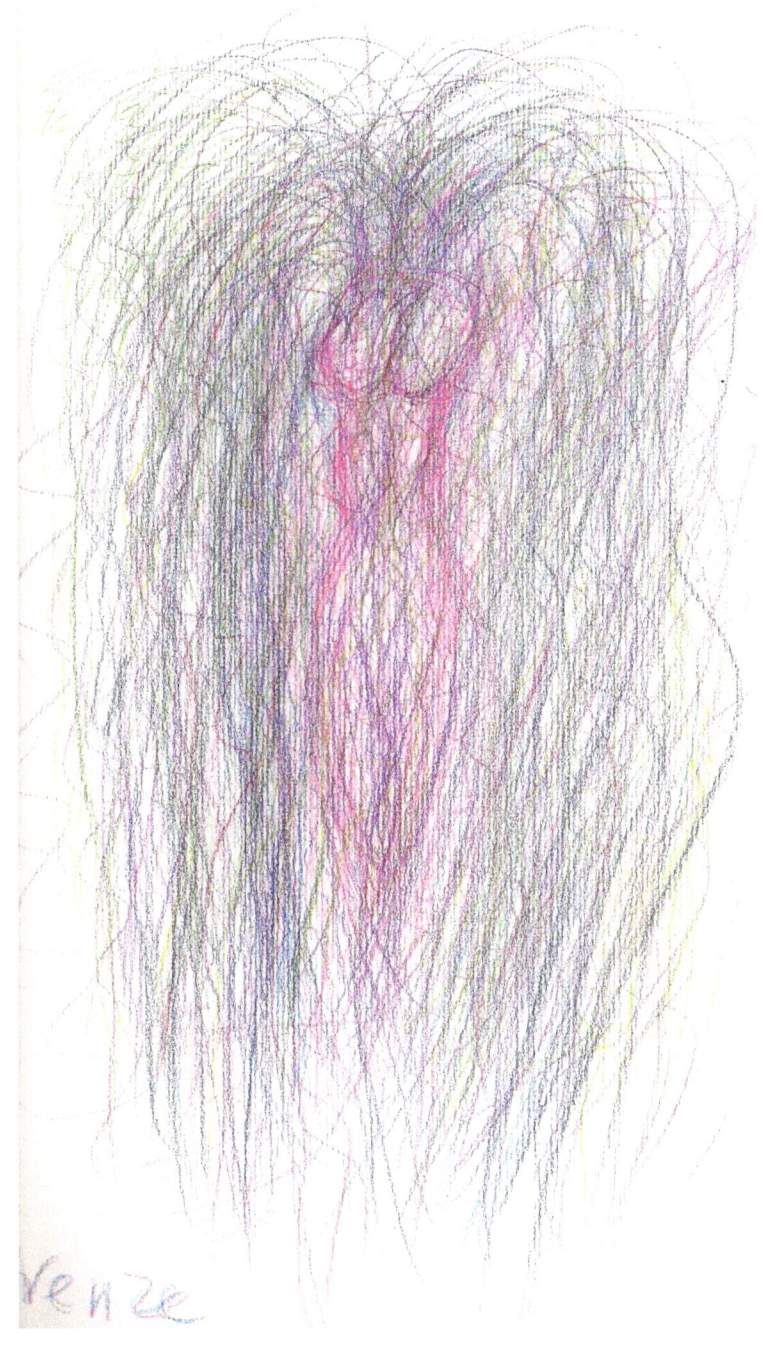

venze

The Goddess of Fruitful Life on the   last

day of 2009 in Florence (M.L. Alonso)

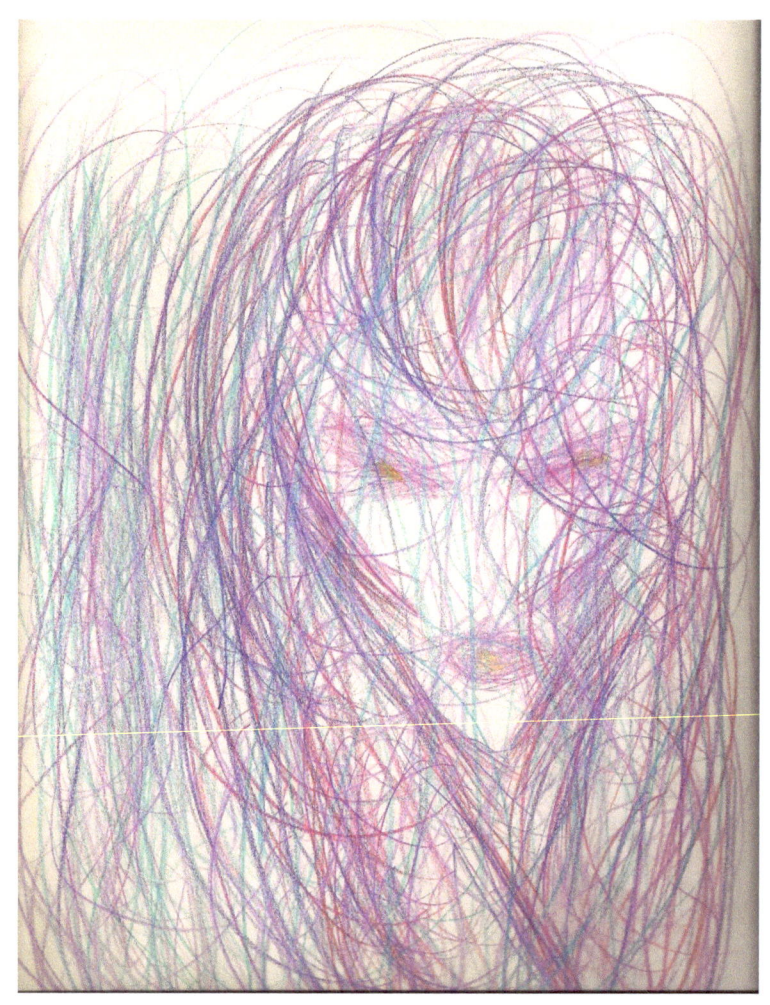

Imbolc (M.I. Alonso)

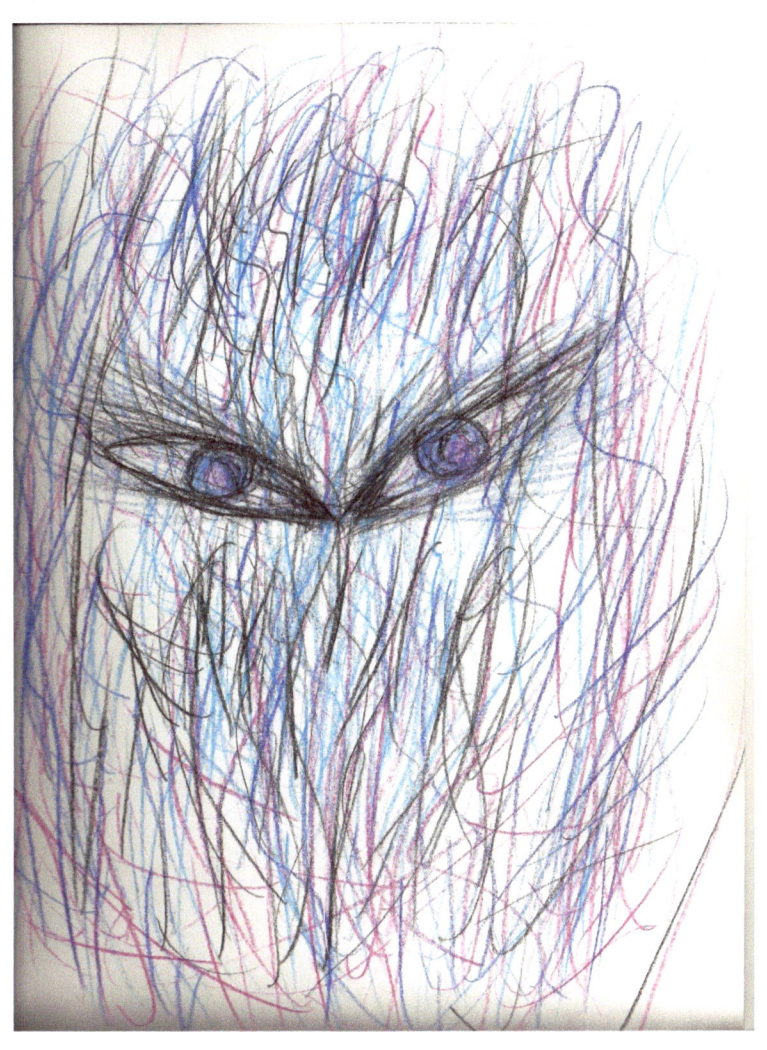

The Goddess' Dark Magical Force

(M.L Alonso)

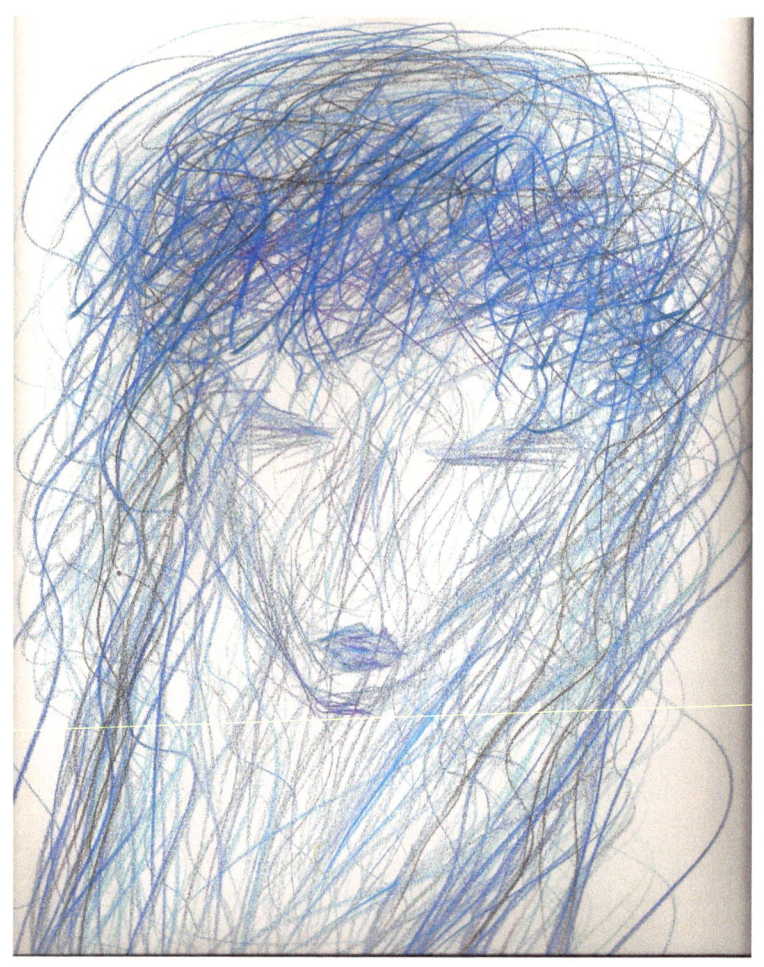

Mater Dolorosa —The Mournful Face of the Goddess. (M.L.Alonso)

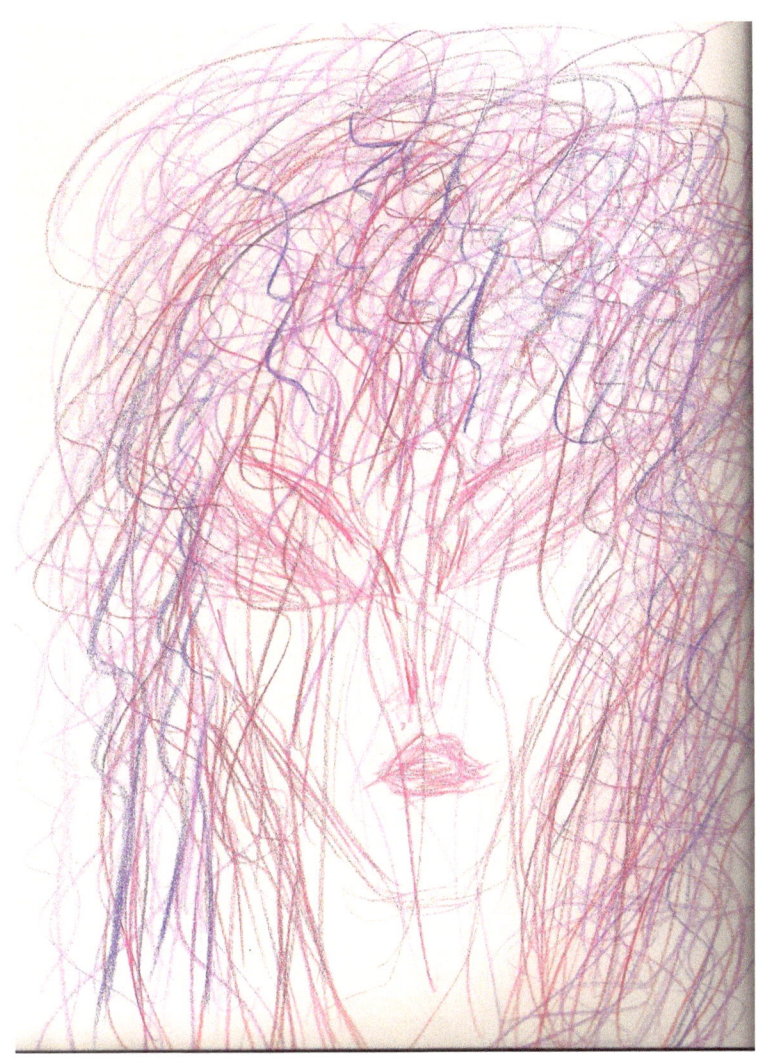

The Dark Side of the Mournful Mother

(M.L.Alonso)

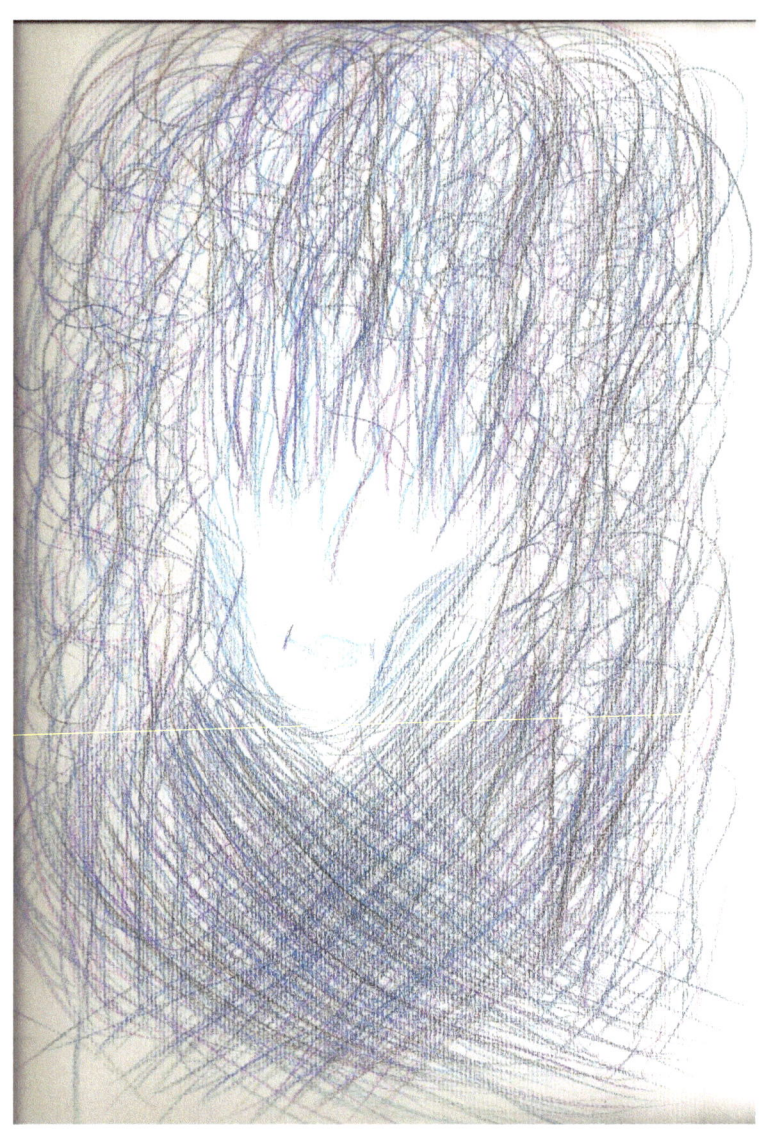

Mors vincit mortis (The Goddess of Death also has a smiling face) (M. L. Alonso)

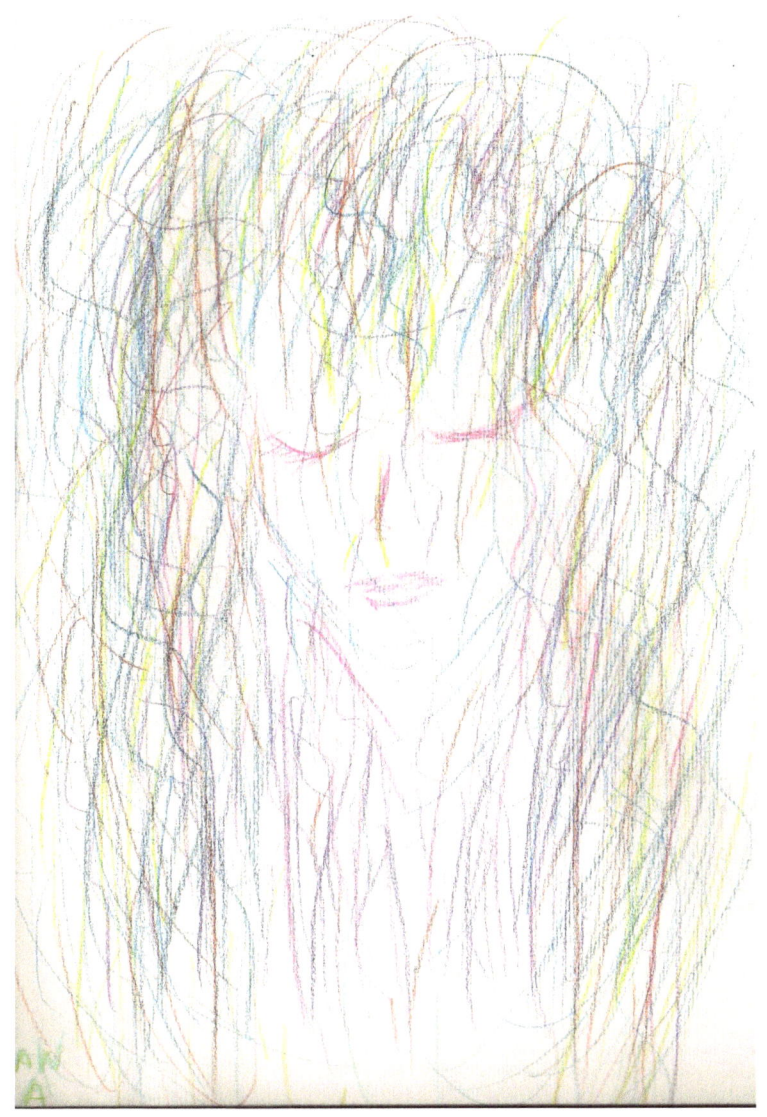

Befana (M.L.Alonso)

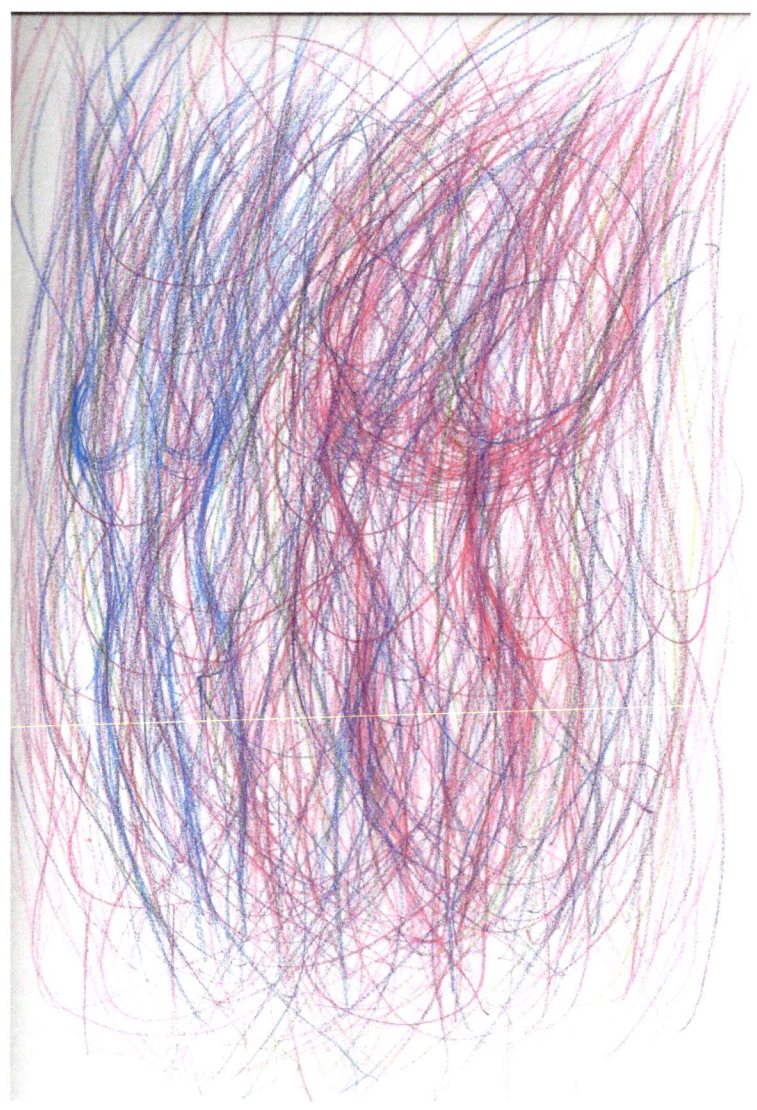

Beltaine (M. L. Alonso)

www.ingramcontent.com/pod-product-compliance
Lightning Source LLC
Chambersburg PA
CBHW041304180526
45172CB00003B/963